PARENTING
from the
PERIPHERY

Dale W. DePalatis

Published by CreateSpace, North Charleston, South Carolina. Printed in the United States of America First Edition, 2018

First Edition publication through Kindle Direct Publishing ISBN: 9781794449374

Layout: D. DePalatis & C. DePalatis
Cover Design: D. DePalatis & C. DePalatis

For inquiries about this book, please contact us:
www.yourglobalfamily.com
Email: dale@yourglobalfamily.com
Facebook.com/yourglobalfam
Instagram: @yourglobalfamily
Twitter: @yourglobalfam

DEDICATION

To Caroline, my beautiful wife, companion, spiritual
sister, lover, friend, partner, editor, and co-adventurer in this
journey of life.

CONTENTS

Preface

1   The Reality of the Situation   1

2   The Adolescent Brain   8

3   Parenting from the Periphery   12

4   Feeding the Limbic System in a Healthy Way   20

5   One Other Healthy Dopamine Option   28

6   Mentors Make a Difference   33

7   Talking with Teens   37

8   Right Reactions   41

9   Limbic Lows   49

10   When Do You Leave the Periphery?   56

Final Thoughts   69

Study Questions   72

Preface

I am not a psychologist, or a sociologist, or a psychiatrist. I don't hold a PhD in Human Behavior or Education or Child Psychology.

I am, however, a high school teacher and a parent. Over a 30-year career teaching English, I have observed a lot of kids with their parents, and I have informally counseled a large number of disturbed parents who are upset because their son or daughter has been acting strangely and isn't listening to them. I have also navigated the often tumultuous waters of parenting three middle school and high school children of my own. I have seen what works with teenagers and what doesn't work. These are my credentials.

I intend this to be a short book with a few important principles that will be of value to you as parents. I believe the ideas in this book can potentially help you succeed in protecting your children from harm, and, in addition, you just might develop a much better relationship with your kids, both in the teen years and as they grow into adults.

The Reality of the Situation

The best of times, the worst of times

Being 12-16 years old stinks. It's a strange period of time when kids are changing radically. Small children turn into gawky teens in a period of what seems like days. Boys sometimes grow 8-12 inches in a year. Girls start their periods. Sexual hormones begin to course through their bodies. Facial hair and cracking voices, pimples, growing pains– in this unsightly state, the desire to impress that guy or girl across the classroom aisle increases in confusing ways. At middle or junior high school, kids leave the relative safety of the individual elementary school classroom with 30 students and move to a larger school fed by several elementary schools with six or seven period days where they wander from class to class, immersed in a weird type of anonymity, unsure of whether all these new people like them or not. It's also the time when kids can potentially come in contact with drugs, alcohol and tobacco which can have negative health effects.

Being 12-16 years old also rocks! Kids get involved with sports or music or a new hobby. They meet cool middle school or high school teachers who give them a vision of the kind of adult they could become. Their bodies slowly find coordination, and they're able to do things they weren't able to do before, whether that's running a 55 second 400 meters or playing a violin concerto. They meet new friends who challenge their thinking and break them out of the small worlds that their families have given them growing up. (Whether it is healthy or unhealthy, the family's world is smaller and more limited than the world kids experience as they progress into middle and high school.) Being 12-16 rocks in a lot of ways.

This is the age where kids need to differentiate from parents and become independent. Instead of the guidance of their parents, the voices of their peer group become more prominent to the child. They are trying to figure out who they are apart from their parents. What will they believe? What kind of person do they want to be? Do they want to be like their parents or different from them?

Being 12-16 years of age is messy, exciting, awkward, rewarding, difficult, confusing, potentially dangerous and transformational. That's the reality of the student's situation. There's a second reality, though. That of the parents.

We parents are in charge here!

Parents have just come through the elementary years with their children. Ages 6-11 are the memory-making years. Although parents need a lot of energy when kids are 6-11, the kids love to spend time with them. They cuddle, wrestle, and play board games with their parents. They love it when mom or dad comes to help out in the elementary school classroom. They absorb like a sponge whatever time the parent gives, and, if dad and/or mom gives them the time they desire, they idolize the parent in return.

Then middle school starts. Suddenly kids are asking parents not to come to their classroom to give them their lunch when they forget it.

"Just leave it at the office. I'll pick it up later."

Instead of cuddles, parents get disgruntled, smelly, grumbling mini-adults who won't get out of bed and have earbuds in 24-7.

Even worse, when parents tell the kids what is happening on the weekend, the kids whine and grumble.

"What happened? The kids never grumbled about our friends coming over for dinner in the past."

"They're your friends, not mine."

"You'll be civil and do what I tell you!" is often how parents respond at this stage.

The reality is that kids are becoming adults. That's a good thing. Parents should not resist this change, but encourage it; however, they are used to their kids doing what they tell them to do, going where they tell them to go, and coming home when they're told to come home.

Parents are used to making all the decisions for young children, but adolescents want to be part of the decision-making process.

Asking for a teen's input on family plans is not

something that comes naturally to many parents, and parents have a hard time changing this mindset. After all, it took a lot of time to teach the kids to obey when they were young

"My kids should do what I tell them to do. We parents are in charge here!"

Other problem attitudes

Not only do parents have a hard time letting their kids have their own opinions and desires related to where they go and what they do, some parents have a very hard time letting their children make decisions about their futures.

I have seen parents who, when they were young, attended an elite college or experienced a major rejection to a preferred college. They now push their kids to become perfectionists so that their school records are impeccable in order to attain admission to that elite or preferred school. These kind of parents pay for expensive summer programs at select universities hoping to pad the resume in such a way that their children will get into that college they attended or wished they could have attended.

I have seen parents who start their kids in baseball when they are three years old, personally coach them, spend every summer of their lives with travel teams, and are now planning their kids' careers in Major League Baseball without ever asking their children if they even enjoy baseball.

I have seen parents who push their kids into certain academic programs because "everyone in the family"

4

is a doctor or a lawyer without ever having observed that their child has not only a love for, but a real talent for writing or computer animation or some other area of interest.

Now, before I go any further, let me say that it's important and right for parents to want the best for their children. Helping children develop academically so they can enter a prestigious college is not a bad thing. Neither is encouraging a kid's athletic potential or facilitating the opportunity to follow in the family footsteps. The problems arise when parents push their agenda on their child without really listening to the child's thoughts on the issue. The reality is that your child is an autonomous being who needs to make his or her own choices in life.

Over my teaching career, I literally can't count how many times I have talked with kids who feel stressed and angry (or sometimes just depressed) due to parents not listening to their thoughts, not taking into account their interests. They feel they have no choice in what happens in their own lives. They say their parents "never" listen to what they want. A common phrase I've heard over and over again through the years is "They've never asked me...."

"They've never asked me what I want." "They've never asked me what I'm interested in." "They've never asked me if I even like the field of medicine!"

It's natural and good that parents should have a lot of input into the choices their children make. A healthy parent-child relationship will lead to a lot of give and take, with the child often asking for the parent's advice. If parents try to live their lives through their children, however, they are in danger of alienating their child or, even worse, driving them into depression or other stress-related illness.

Another problem lies in the area of protectiveness. Parents have more experience in life than their children and have wisdom attained through that experience. Some parents learned things "the hard way" and want to protect their children from making the same mistakes.

The problem with this mindset is that the individual child needs to experience his or her own mistakes and learn from them.

"I know what will happen if you go out with that group of boys. You'll only get into trouble."

"When I was your age, I really messed myself up by eating too much junk food. In this house, you'll only be eating organic vegetables."

"I had a really bad experience with drugs at a live concert. You're not going to go to any concerts while you're under my roof."

Disobedience or dissent in the protective family is often not allowed. The child feels stifled and, ironically, is sometimes even motivated to do the things that are prohibited just because they are prohibited.

Consider three homes with big glass windows in the front. One of them has a big sign that reads, "Don't throw rocks through the window!" Which home's windows do you think will get broken?

There is something in the human psyche that wants to experience that which is prohibited; when parents place lots of prohibitions on the developing teen, the teen is much more likely to want to experience what is prohibited, especially since this is a time period when kids are questioning whether they want to be like their parents or not.

"What would it be like to disobey? Do I like junk food better than health food? Will hanging out with those people really ruin my life? Going to a live concert sounds like fun!"

That's the reality of the situation. Kids need to differentiate and grow up. Parents have a hard time letting them.

The Adolescent Brain

If parents want to learn to effectively deal with their newly recalcitrant differentiating teen, they need to be aware of how the adolescent brain functions. Once again, I'm not a brain expert, but, as an educator, I have attended lots of conferences and in-services that inform us about the latest research as it relates to adolescent development. So the following information, though gleaned through the ears of an amateur, has research backing.

The prefrontal cortex

First of all, whether they know it or not, all parents want their children to develop their prefrontal cortex. This is the area of the brain that is located at the front of the head where personality develops. It's the area where reasoning and planning takes place, but it also does not fully develop until about age 25.

The prefrontal cortex is associated with

judgment, decision making, and mental flexibility—or with the ability to change plans when faced with an obstacle," explained Cecilia Flores, senior author on the study and professor at McGill [University's] Department of Psychiatry. She adds, "Its functioning is important for learning, motivation, and cognitive processes. Given its prolonged development into adulthood, this region is particularly susceptible to being shaped by life experiences in adolescence, such as stress and drugs of abuse. Such alterations in prefrontal cortex development can have long-term consequences later on in life. (Bergland)

If the prefrontal cortex develops smoothly, students can grow into successful adults who are able to deal with complicated tasks, make plans, change plans, evaluate situations, and make their ways through life with mental flexibility.

There is a problem, however.

Adolescents are addicts.

In fact, every human is an addict. All people are addicted to the happiness hormones found in the limbic system further back in the brain: oxytocin, endorphin, serotonin and dopamine. When humans cuddle, oxytocin is produced, creating a warm and comfortable feeling. A runner experiences the "runner's high" which is actually the result of endorphin (a substance that is chemically very similar to morphine). Exercise can also induce

9

the release of serotonin, another feel-good hormone. Behaviors like friendship, bungee jumping or posting on social media, elicit a squirt of another hormone called dopamine that makes us feel great, but risky behaviors like drug abuse, premarital sex or gambling also flush the body with dopamine.

Adolescents are especially sensitive to dopamine squirts. Since the adolescent brain is still developing, there is evidence that dopamine affects adolescents more strongly than adults. In other words, nothing will ever feel as good as it does during adolescence (sorry, parents!). Not only does this make risky behavior attractive to adolescents, it also causes them to be easily addicted to the behavior. The more dopamine that is released, the more a person wants to repeat that behavior.

There is also one thing that appears to be a producer of dopamine in adolescents that doesn't produce dopamine in adults: proximity to peers. Not only does just being near peers produce dopamine, but risky behaviors with peers produce optimal amounts of the dopamine high.

Laurence Steinberg, Psychology Professor at Temple University, talks about the peer factor in dopamine production in his book *Age of Opportunity: Lessons from the New Science of Adolescence*:

> This explains why teenagers are more reckless when they are with their friends. During adolescence, peers light up the same reward centers that are aroused by drugs, sex, food, and money. Adolescents get a dopamine squirt from being with their friends, just as they do

from other things that make them feel good. It's true in adolescent rodents as well as human adolescents. Being around animals the same age is so rewarding during adolescence that socializing with peers provokes chemical changes in the adolescent rodent's brain–but not the adult's brain– that are similar to those seen when the animals are given alcohol! (98)

Because of this hormone reward for peer interaction, teenagers during this critical stage of development crave hanging out with peers like an alcoholic craves alcohol.

In other words, parents are not going to be able to stop their teenagers from desiring the presence of their peers. They are receiving both psychological and physiological benefit from being around them. In a way, they are addicted to peer interaction (and, as a corollary, not interested in parent interaction).

So, kids need to differentiate, parents want them to listen to them, but they are literally addicted to interaction with their peer group.

What's a Parent to Do?

The thing parents need to do, therefore, is discover a way to influence that peer interaction. To do so, however, they need to be skillful and a bit clandestine. It's a little like being an undercover agent in the teenage world.

This background information leads to the core idea of this book and the key parenting skill needed to successfully navigate this strange period of adolescent life: parenting from the periphery.

Parenting from the Periphery

The basic idea of parenting from the periphery is that parents need to retreat into the background, giving kids more freedom and opportunity to make decisions, thereby giving them the *opportunity* to fail, but patrolling the periphery of the child's life to prevent them from doing anything really stupid.

Does this mean parents should just let teens do whatever they want? No! After all, the teen's prefrontal cortex is not yet developed, so they benefit from a mature person whose cortex is already developed giving them some attention. Madeline Levine, a PhD in Psychology whom I heard speak at a Challenge Success conference, calls this giving the teenager an "ancillary brain." Especially when teens are getting dopamine highs from being with their peers and entertaining the idea of risky behavior, it's essential for parents to do the work of parenting and exercise the role of the ancillary brain for their children.

That being said, teenagers don't like the parent

12

as ancillary brain telling them what to do. Parents, therefore, need to give kids freedom to fail within the periphery of certain boundaries, but they also have to do the hard work of paying attention to what's going on with them. Parents need to quietly keep an eye on where their kids are going, what they're doing, and who their friends are while at the same time not letting the interest seem too overt.

If teens start to feel that their parents are hanging around them too much or are becoming helicopter parents, they will resent it. The skillful parent shows interest when the child is open to sharing, but also doesn't push when the child isn't interested in sharing.

So what does this look like in real life?

Grades

One area where parenting from the periphery is essential as kids get older is in the area of schoolwork. Adolescents need to learn how to manage their own work and meet deadlines without anyone holding their hands, and yet, as these skills develop, students may occasionally need parental help.

So how do you do that from the periphery? Modern technology helps in this area. Most schools have online grading programs that allow a parent to see how kids are doing in their classes. Don't use these programs to micromanage your child's education, but just keep an eye on them to be aware of any patterns. If a large number of missing assignments start piling up or lots of "F's" begin to appear, it's time to ask how they're doing in classes. See if there is anything they need in order to succeed, but always place the onus of their education on them and their effort.

"I noticed you've had some poor grades on Biology tests. What's your plan to pull your grade up in that class?" is better than "You're grounded until you get that grade up!"

Instead of focusing purely on the grades, talk about the learning. "How are you feeling about that AP History class? Are you connecting with the teacher all right? What's the hardest thing for you in that class?" If your child is in a communicative mood, you may end up having an adult conversation about their learning and be able to offer some suggestions. Be careful, though. If the child doesn't want to talk, just let them be, but try again when they're in a better mood.

Romantic relationships

In the area of romantic relationships, peripheral parenting is emotionally hard to do. If parents see an unhealthy relationship developing, it's easy to feel like you want to jump in and protect your child! However, instead, parents need to find ways to subtly discourage the negative relationship without taking away all the choices from their child.

As an example, our daughter Erika started getting interested in a boy in her freshman year of high school. She was 14 years old, and it was her first romantic relationship. The boy was good looking and an athlete, but we weren't totally sure whether he was trustworthy. We may have just been freaking out because this was the first time we'd encountered this situation, but our gut feeling was to be cautious.

Rather than doing what we felt like doing – i.e. prohibiting the relationship completely – we allowed her to go with him to some specific places that always included being with others (like over to our house for lunch, to events for the cross country team or to church, etc.). Since she didn't have her license, we made sure we drove her to and from the meetings.

We also sought wise advice from some friends we admire who had older children to navigate this challenge. Their input proved key, and led to us discussing with our daughter some valuable dating and relationship principles for our family.

Still, we gave her a good degree of space. This limited freedom gave her time to get her prefrontal cortex into play, and, in the end, through some heartache, she made good decisions about the relationship.

This is an area that requires discernment, especially with younger teens. Since there is danger of pregnancy, STDs, etc., parents sometimes need to step inside the periphery a little more.

Money

Parenting from the periphery should also apply in the area of money. Many parents give allowances to young kids, but they control when kids go to the store, whether they can use their money, and what specifically they are allowed to buy. As kids enter adolescence, however, parents need to let them decide how to use their money.

My two sons have always loved Lego. When my

eldest son Justin was twelve, he became interested in buying a large and expensive Lego Dino-Attack Helicopter. It would cost the entire contents of his savings account. When he was younger, I would have told him that it was too expensive. Now, the conversation went like this:

"It's my money, Dad! Why can't I use it like I want?"

"You're right. It is your money, but have you considered how you will pay for your brother's birthday present next month or Christmas presents this year if you spend all your money on the helicopter?"

"I'll wash the cars."

"Getting $5 here or there will not refill your account."

"But I really want it! It's my money!"

"You're right. You need to manage your money, so make a wise decision."

He bought the helicopter and experienced some real problems because he didn't even have money for basic necessities. A few years later when he wanted to buy an expensive guitar, he remembered that situation and waited to buy the guitar until his bank account could handle the stress. As a parent, it was hard letting him do something we knew was foolish, but we resisted bailing him out because he needed to learn that financial lesson.

If young people aren't given responsibility for money early on, they may have lots of financial difficulties as they learn to negotiate life in the real world.

Going out with Friends

In the area of going out with friends, parenting from the periphery can also get a little complicated. It's the unsupervised parties at friends' houses where a lot of the risk taking with drugs, alcohol and sex take place. Once adolescents have their driver's licenses, they are going to want to be out and about, and late nights with peers and dopamine can lead to negative consequences.

Parents need to draw some of the boundaries long before their kids get their licenses. Examples of those boundaries might include no parties at homes without parental supervision, no borrowing of the car without details of where the child is going, and no staying out late without a check-in phone call.

Here's an example of a conversation I had with my youngest son Luke when he was 16. We had already established the boundaries:

"Hey, Dad, can I borrow the car tonight?"

"Sure, what's going on?"

"Some friends of mine and I want to go to this trivia night at the pub downtown."

"Do they let underage kids into the pub?"

"Yeah, it's a restaurant, too. Lots of people go to these trivia nights. There's even a group of teachers from our school who compete."

"Okay. What time can we expect you home?"

"10:00 or 10:30."

"Have a great time."

So notice that parenting from the periphery doesn't mean absence of rules for your child. It means embedding opportunities for making choices and the accompanying opportunity to fail within the framework of the boundaries you create. It also can be a little scary for the parent because, for example in the situation above, we gave Luke the opportunity to secretly drink or get involved in some other negative behavior. We trusted him in this situation because of his track record of making good choices.

Realize that each child is different. My son in the example above had already shown himself to be responsible with the car, trustworthy to tell us where he was going and why, and able to go somewhere with his friends and return at the time he said. His friends had also proven to be kids who don't push my son toward risky behavior with drugs or alcohol. If my son had gone out with friends and returned at 2:00 in the morning without calling or if he had tried to deceive us in other areas, there would have been a different conversation:

"Hey, Dad, could I borrow the car tonight?"

"Maybe, but last time you borrowed the car, you said you'd come home at 9:00, and you didn't bring it back until after midnight."

"I know. I just lost track of time."

"A responsible adult needs to keep track of time and return a car that he's borrowed when he says he will."

"I understand. I made that mistake before, and won't make it again."

"All right. We'll give it another try. What's going on tonight?"

Parents need to learn how to make flexible, rather than inflexible, rules. For example, "You have to go to bed every night at 9:00 p.m." is an inflexible rule that is appropriate for the parenting of younger children, but

"You can decide when you go to bed as long as you are able to get out of bed by yourself in the morning and be ready to leave by 7:00 a.m." is more flexible and a better "rule" for a developing adult.

These are just a few examples of situations where parenting from the periphery comes into play. Each family is different, and each relationship with each child is unique, so how it looks in any given situation varies.

The key idea, however, is that the parent is treating the budding adult as an adult. Instead of commands, the parent offers questions and suggestions with the expectation that the child will respond to the parent with respect and adult-like behavior.

You may be thinking at this point, "But the 'budding adult' is truly only budding, and he is still a risk-taking, immature, peer-impressing ball of hormones ready to explode and addicted to dopamine."

That is true, and that's why the idea of parenting from the periphery is not an excuse to relax our attention toward our children. In fact, this type of parenting often requires more energy and thought. Since our kids can easily experience deleterious consequences from bad choices when given some freedom, it's imperative to do anything in your power to nudge your kids toward healthy dopamine-heavy activities rather than allowing them to drift into unhealthy risk-taking behaviors.

Feeding the Limbic System in a Healthy Way

The limbic system hormones are not bad things. In fact, so much of our feelings of happiness and contentment as adults are wrapped up in whether we are getting the right amounts of the right kinds of these feel-good hormones. It's the same with adolescents. Adults get in trouble when they get addicted to the wrong kind of dopamine highs like alcoholism or marital infidelity. Adolescents also get into trouble when they get addicted to the wrong kinds of dopamine highs.

The abuse of alcohol and drugs is always high on the parents' list of worries for their children. In the current milieu of American public schools, kids are going to have the opportunity to try drugs and alcohol at some point. It makes a big difference, however, if they are already getting dopamine highs in other healthier ways.

In other words, one way for parents to help teens avoid risk-taking behavior is to divert them into healthy risk-taking behavior that gives the same reward of dopamine but doesn't involve activities that can lead to

STDs or overdoses.

Feed your kids' limbic hormone hunger with positive risk-taking activities! And yet, you still have to do this subtly in a way that lets the child think it's his or her idea.

If your son shows an interest in camping, ask one of his friends who is a Boy Scout to invite him to a Boy Scouts activity, buy him some cool equipment, etc.

If your daughter likes mountain biking, get her a great bike and introduce her to a cool adult leader of a bike racing team who will invite her to get involved.

Or if she wants to rock climb, pay for it, but stay out of the way and let her feel like she is doing it as an edgy activity.

Any situation that is supervised by adults but gives the child an opportunity for a thrill or the development of a skill or the opportunity to compete in something exciting can feed the limbic rewards without destructive consequences. There are lots of possibilities!

Scouting

My son Justin wandered into a group of friends in elementary school who were interested in scouting, so we worked with a couple of the other parents to start a Cub Scout den, and, when the boys got old enough, they went on to Boy Scouts. Although I was raised with a lot of wilderness activities as a boy growing up in Alaska, we didn't have a scout troop in my area, so I never got involved in that program.

As a high school teacher, however, I am a member of the scholarship committee, and, over the years, we have interviewed many young men who have become

Eagle Scouts through the very active troop in our area. These young men are articulate, intelligent, athletic, and well rounded. When my son got interested in this activity, I was pleased and quietly did everything I could to encourage him, from buying him backpacks and high-tech gear to driving him and his buddies to camps. The troop near us is a scout-led troop, so parents are definitely on the periphery of the activities (the perfect place to be!).

One thing I noticed with all of these Eagle Scouts is that they had internalized a moral code that inoculated them against a lot of the more dangerous risk-taking activities. Although there are probably exceptions, in my experience, I haven't seen Eagle Scouts getting wasted on drugs or facilitating parties at their homes when their parents are away. I think the reason why is that they are getting their dopamine highs from 30-mile hikes, camping, and achieving merit badges on a variety of fascinating topics.

Youth groups

Another group of kids that I've observed over nearly 30 years of public school teaching who appear to have found a healthy dopamine activity is the synagogue or church kids. Specifically, I'm talking about kids who are actively involved in a youth group with meaningful activities.

Our area has several churches and synagogues that do a good job with youth programs. Kids not only get a moral education, but they go on perspective-blowing missions trips and relationship-building camps and a myriad of other character-developing activities led by "cool" adults (i.e. not parents) who are great role models.

I remember one situation where one of my students who had been experimenting with some risky behaviors was asked by a friend to go on the youth group's mission trip to Mexico. There he saw the difficulties that people in the developing world experience and was also able to help out with programs for young kids. He came back enthused about service and got involved with a club at our school that was trying to help build a school for indigent kids in Peru. He was so busy, he didn't ever get back into the risky experimentation he had been doing previously.

In another case, a boy who was known as a party guy, went on a summer youth group houseboat trip. On the trip, he became known as the kid who could do amazing flip dives off the top of the houseboat. He also had some meaningful experiences relating to his peers and discussing deeper life issues. He returned a different person. The healthy diving and relational dopamine highs had replaced some of the riskier activities he had pursued previously.

Academic clubs

Any activity that allows your child to travel with their peers under the supervision of an adult has the potential to give them positive dopamine input. School academic clubs like Robotics, Mock Trial, Model UN, Speech Club, Debate Club, Poetry Club, etc. often have competitions in other places where the group needs to travel as a team for a few days. This time away from parents gives the kids opportunity to make independent choices with their peers while having boundaries set by the advisor or coach.

My daughter Erika became involved with Mock Trial in her junior year of high school. Mock Trial is a club where students compete on the local, state, and even national level to try a fictional legal case. They learn how to do the job of a lawyer, using evidence and knowledge of the law to both prosecute and defend the same case. Some of the kids do the job of lawyers while others play the parts of the defendant, the witnesses, and even the bailiff. Real volunteer judges from the community preside over the contests in real courtrooms, adding a gravitas and authenticity to the activity. Many kids who participate in Mock Trial go on to legal careers.

As my daughter got involved, she loved the camaraderie of preparing for the trial. She worked with her teammates to prepare perfect openings, cross examinations and closing statements. As they traveled around the state to various competitions, a real bond formed with her companions around this healthy activity. Her coach was a former lawyer turned teacher who was a wonderful role model and pushed the kids to do their best job. Standing up in front of judges and competing for a State Championship provided plenty of dopamine so that they had no need for any riskier stuff!

In fact, the wave of dopamine that hit me as a peripheral parent chaperone when my daughter's team came in 6th in State (our school had never come in higher than 11th previously) was strong enough to make me high for several days. For the kids that buzz probably lasted a year!

Musical groups

And then there's music! If your budding adult has any interest in playing an instrument or singing or starting a band, encourage it! Just listening to music is a powerful dopamine producer, so being involved in the creation of beauty yourself is a thrill whether it's playing the cello in the school orchestra, singing the baritone part in the choir or pulling off a complicated electric guitar riff in a rock band.

Music was one of the things that fed my dopamine engine when I was in high school. I sang in an acapella jazz ensemble, a concert choir, and a barbershop quartet during my secondary education. One year I was chosen for All-Northwest Honor Choir and went to Seattle for a concert with 120 of the best high school singers from six states. Directed by a famous conductor, the singers of this choir could hit every note and every cut-off perfectly. We sang one song that had a huge crescendo that led to a beautiful fortissimo chord that then cut to absolute silence. Then the voices re-entered to finish the piece. In our final practice before the concert, when the choir crescendoed to the huge chord and cut off, the silence was so beautiful that we all held our breath waiting for the conductor to continue as electricity ran up and down our spines. But he didn't continue. He dropped his hands and didn't even finish the piece. "You're ready," he said and walked off the stage. Just thinking about that moment many years later gives me a huge jolt of joy.

A word about sports

Sports are a huge part of our society. As a high school teacher, I watch so many kids who delight in the strength and flexibility of their bodies and have high hopes of pushing themselves to great athletic accomplishments. Many who aren't even superstar athletes dream of one day becoming professionals. Most are deluding themselves since very few people actually make it to the professional ranks in sports. Nevertheless, just as professional athletes claim rewards of wealth and fame in the larger world, athletes in high school tend to be more popular and therefore have potential to face more temptations in the areas of partying and destructive risk-taking behaviors.

Participating in sports as an activity is a great way to get healthy dopamine rewards. The discipline required to practice hours each day, get in shape, and perform at a high level can transfer into other areas of life, like work and relationships. The camaraderie of working with a team also leads to the development of important collaboration skills, and the influence of a good coach can have lifelong impact.

Being aware of the popularity factor with sports, though, should lead parents to keep extra watch around social activities and warrants other types of creative parenting. Our high school, for example, has a special voluntary drug-testing program for athletes. When an athlete signs up for the program, he or she will be randomly drug tested several times during the school year. Although the testing isn't consistent enough to be sure kids are staying away from drugs, the real value of the program is giving conscientious students an excuse when, due to their athletic popularity, their friends push them to participate in risky behavior with alcohol or drugs.

"No, sorry. My parents signed me up for drug testing, so I can't risk doing anything. I might get thrown off the team."

The idea that a child will become a professional athlete also deludes some parents. It's a wonderful dream to think of your child competing on a national stage and drawing the huge salary that a professional baseball or football player can command. Just make sure that your child knows that it's a longshot! If you have the talent to potentially become a professional, realize that injury can also derail promising careers. That is why it is imperative to have a Plan B if you're working toward an athletic career.

As a parent attempting to guide your teen from the periphery, you shouldn't decide for your child that they can't try for a career in sports, but you can fill their lives with a diversity of opportunities that will develop in them a variety of interests and skills. If the athletic dream fails, the child will then have some other capabilities to fall back on.

One final point about sports. Go to the games. Don't scream too loud or draw attention to yourself. Don't try to coach your kid. Just be there. Your kids won't tell you this, but it matters to them that you're there.

Another Healthy Dopamine Option

One other option for developing a healthy dopamine addiction I'd like to suggest is something that our family did. We went overseas with our family for a year!

My wife and I have always been interested in international things. My wife Caroline grew up with Japanese exchange students in her home and was an international relations major as an undergraduate, then completed an M.A. in Japanese-English translation and interpretation.

I focused on European languages, especially Italian and German, during my undergraduate years, but mysteriously got interested in Asia when I met my future wife… . This led me to study Japanese and learn about Asian cultures.

During our college years, both of us studied abroad, she in Japan and I in Italy. Then, after marriage, we worked in Japan for a couple of years and later traveled throughout Asia.

We had always envisioned raising our kids overseas,

but what actually happened was we got involved in an organization that reaches out to help international students in the U.S. That involvement fed our interest in other cultures, so, after Caroline's grad school, we stayed put in our current hometown of Monterey, California to start our family.

Fast forward 15 years, and we found ourselves never having taken our kids to live for any extended time overseas, and the kids were entering the "uncooperative" age I'm describing in this book.

An objection

Before I continue this story, let me attempt to head off an objection. You may be thinking, "These two had all this background in international relations and languages. I, however, know nothing about other cultures and have no ability with languages. This isn't something I can do."

If this is your feeling, realize that no one is really prepared to go overseas, no matter how much cultural study and/or language learning they've done. It's always a shock to leave your own culture and way of doing things to go to a strange place with different foods, transportation systems, and language. But, in some ways, that's the point.

By leaving the comfort zone,, you put yourselves in the "high-dopamine" mode. Everything is different, so you're seeing, smelling, hearing new things every day. In one sense, the best prerequisite for moving your family overseas is to have no experience with international things. It will just make the dopamine highs higher.

So, on with the story…

We began to explore options for going overseas. International programs abound from short-term (2-3 months) volunteer opportunities to getting a job and living someplace for a year or more.

We first decided to apply for a Fulbright Teacher Exchange program since I, as a public school teacher, could get a sabbatical from my job for a year, and we also needed to make some income while overseas to make this financially possible. The Fulbright program accepted me to be a U.S. exchange teacher in Turkey. At the last minute, however, this fell through since they couldn't find a comparable high school teacher in Turkey to complete the exchange.

After a lot of scrambling and sending of resumes, we learned of an opportunity in Ningbo, China where both my wife and I could teach at a university. This would let us earn enough money to support our living costs in China, so we signed the contract and began the preparations to take a year off from our ordinary U.S. life.

You can imagine that our kids had varying reactions to this adventure. With 8-year-old Luke, 12-year-old Erika, and 14-year-old Justin, their emotions swayed from excitement to terror, but, even in the preparation, we were all getting dopamine highs.

Given what I've already said in this book, you might think it wasn't the smartest thing to take a 14-year-old boy out of his peer group of friends, take him to a foreign country, then stick him in a small apartment with the parents from whom he was trying to differentiate and his two kid siblings. Yet the pressure of adapting to a new environment and learning how to function in a new culture formed a unique bond within our family.

We were also able to connect our children with mentors in China. For Justin, it was a teacher at the Chinese school he was attending. Chen-Laoshi took Justin under her wing and made it her project to help him not only learn Chinese, but also feel comfortable in the school. Erika and Luke developed relationships with some of the university students we were teaching, and that helped them navigate life in Ningbo.

Now don't get me wrong. Life in China was not just a comfortable series of wonderful experiences. Each child had struggles in different ways. Justin, in particular (as might be expected due to his being in the center of the age group we're discussing), had big mood swings and times of depression. There were even times when we wondered if it had been the right decision to move our family overseas.

In retrospect, however, this year abroad became a watershed event in the life of our family. Not only did it give us a shared fund of memories, it developed a resilience and strength in each of our children and broke them out of the narrow rut of American life.

Despite their initial hesitancy and in-country struggles, all three of our kids have talked about how significant that experience was in their development and are glad we took the trip.

It also provided a year of nonstop healthy dopamine highs that I believe prevented our children from getting into unhealthy risk-taking situations. If you're interested in hearing more about our adventures, check out my wife's book *Jumping Out of the Mainstream: An American Family's Year Abroad,* available on Amazon.

Notice that a common denominator keeps coming up in these examples of healthy hormone activities: the presence of a mentor, coach, teacher, or other responsible adult.

Mentors Make a Difference

In adolescence, kids care more about their peers' input than their parents'. I have no scientific evidence of this, but I believe there is some kind of inhibitory hormone that prevents kids from hearing their parents' voices between the ages of 12-16. The strange thing is that this hormone just affects the kids' ability to hear the voices of their parents; they can hear other adults' voices.

That's why it's so important to subtly encourage your child to find a mentor.

The reason I know this is because, over many years of teaching, I have been that other adult whom children can hear. As a high school English teacher, I have spoken numerous times with parents who ask me to communicate something to their children. The conversations go something like this:

"I have tried to tell Andy to do his homework before dinner, but he won't listen to me. Is there anything you can do?"

Later on I have a conversation with Andy.

"So, Andy, you haven't been getting your reading done lately. What's up?"

"I want to do it, but I keep falling asleep while I'm reading."

"When are you reading?"

"While I'm lying in bed before I go to sleep."

"That doesn't sound like it's the best time to have an alert mind for reading. Why don't you try reading first thing after you get home, maybe before dinner while you're still alert and awake?"

"All right. I'll try."

A few days later, mom calls me.

"What did you do? He's doing all his homework right after he gets home without complaining!"

"I think he hears me better than you."

It's true. Budding adults want to feel like they're adults. They hear the voices of many adults around them and want to be like them. The two adults in their lives that they literally can't hear are their mother and father because the life task they're working at right now is differentiation from their parents.

Parents should not get discouraged, however, thinking that they're the only adults that their kids don't want to be like. The fact is that you are your child's baseline idea of what an adult is. Even while ignoring your voice, your child is comparing the way you do things to the way other adults do things to decide if they want to be like you or like the other adult. When your child has fully developed his or her adult persona, you will find that a good percentage of that persona will be modeled on the parents' character. (That could be a good or a scary thing….)

When trying to find a mentor for your child, do it subtly; try to find someone your child is already gravitating toward and quietly encourage the relationship, then get to know that person yourself and enlist the mentor's aid to be your child's "ancillary brain" as Madeline Levine would say.

In our family, the mentors for our kids have been teachers, coaches, Boy Scout leaders, and church Youth leaders.

During my eldest son's career in Boy Scouts, there were various times when he got discouraged in the pursuit of the ultimate goal of reaching Eagle Scout. At one point right after we returned from China where he had spent a year making no progress on his scouting goals, he felt like there were just too many merit badges to get done.

I looked over what he still had to do, and, though there was a lot of work involved, I had a conversation with him and outlined a way he could get it done bit by bit over a period of six months or so.

He did nothing. I don't think my plan even registered in his brain.

Later I had another talk with him and suggested he try to finish a certain number of merit badges at a summer camp.

At the camp, he did a few badges, but not the ones I had suggested. When I asked him about it, he told me to quit bugging him about it. He said he was in control of it, and I shouldn't worry.

Then one evening I found myself standing next to his Scout Leader as I waited for a scouting event to finish. Sam and I made some small talk, then he asked me how Justin was doing on his advancement to Eagle.

"Okay, I guess. He doesn't seem to be doing the right badges, though, to make the progress he needs to make."

"Really? Well, maybe I could go over the requirements with him."

"That would be awesome!"

A few weeks later Justin told me he was giving a speech at the meeting.

"I'm finishing up the Citizenship in the Community badge."

"Isn't that one of the ones we talked about finishing last summer?"

"I don't remember, but I had a talk with Sam last week, and he showed me how I could finish it up quickly. We have a plan for me to finish all my merit badges for Eagle by next summer. I think I can do this."

He went on to complete his Eagle Scout badge thanks to the voice of a mentor.

Talking with Teens

In addition to encouraging your children to have healthy mentors, another thing we parents need to do is learn how to speak with our children differently when they enter the teen years.

How you speak with your teenager has a huge impact on how your teenager responds to you. This is an area where parents really struggle. After all, for the first ten years of the child's life, you have been speaking with your child like this:

"Alex, it's time to go to school now. Get up. I have breakfast on the kitchen table for you. Come downstairs right away."

"Okay, kids, we'll be going to Colorado for Spring Break. Since we have to drive to Tahoe by noon, we'll need to leave by 8:00 a.m. Be ready to go."

"Gabriella, that was not a nice thing to do. You share with your friend!"

There's nothing wrong with talking with young children like this. In fact, parents have a responsibility to care for their kids, set boundaries for them, discipline them, and get them to the places they need to go.

The problem arises, however, when your child enters the stage that we've been talking about in this book. First of all, as stated in the last chapter, your child can barely hear your voice, so anything you say may not even register in the kid's conscious mind. Secondly, the budding adult doesn't want to be told what to do.

Think about it. How often do you go up to a colleague at work and say, "Diego, we're going out to lunch in ten minutes. You can either have a hamburger or some pasta, but not both. Be ready to leave, so I don't have to wait for you."

Instead, your conversation probably goes more like this:

"Hey, Diego. Do you want to go out for lunch today? What do you feel like eating? How about trying that new burger place in the Atrium? Would leaving in ten minutes work for you?"

Asking, not telling

Notice the big difference between those two conversations. Adults tell kids what to do but ask other adults to participate in the decision making.

If you learn just one thing from this book, what I'm talking about here has the potential to radically transform the effectiveness of your relating with your adolescent child.

Ask them to *participate in decision making*, and they will start responding to you like an adult. Speak to your kids like adults. Instead of commanding them to do something, talk it over with them.

"Good morning, Alex. I'm making myself some eggs; would you like some? Anything I can do to help you get going?"

"Mom and I have been talking over the idea of going to Colorado for Spring Break. What do you kids think? The other option that might be possible is a visit to the Grand Canyon, but we want your input. Any thoughts?"

"Mom and I like that lunch restaurant in Tahoe. Do you have enough time this evening to get packed, so we could all get out of here by 8:00 tomorrow morning? If we leave by 8:00, we can make it there by noon."

"Gabriella, relationships are important things. If I were you, I would reconsider how I'm treating my friends."

Respect is key

In each of these examples, the parent is inviting the child to participate in the decision-making process. Instead of feeling like a slave who has to do whatever the master says, the child feels like his or her voice is important to the parent.

A simple way to check whether you're doing this right is to ask yourself, "Would I talk to an adult friend with these words?" If the answer is "no," then think of what you would say to the adult friend and use those words.

If you as a parent can make the switch from talking *to* your adolescent like a child to talking *with* your adolescent like an adult, you will establish a healthy mode of communication.

At the root of this type of communication is respect. This is also one of our goal as parents, right? We want to raise children who are worthy of respect. If parents regularly show respect to their children, the children grow up wanting to be worthy of that respect.

Respecting your children will help you and them navigate the turgid tributary of adolescence and will continue to facilitate meaningful communication between parent and child into the tumultuous tides of adulthood.

Right Reactions

How you talk with your child is not the only peripheral parenting skill that has an influence on the way he or she relates to you. The other thing is how you react to your child's failures.

When a child does something impulsive, risky, or acts without thinking, do you blow up? Ground them? Give them a lecture? Do you overreact to a situation that doesn't warrant such an overreaction?

As an adult, you have a fully developed prefrontal cortex. You don't need to respond with wild overreaction. In other words, don't be surprised when your child does something completely idiotic; don't get upset. This is the power of the wild and beautiful adaptations working in their bodies that they have no control over. The hormones will lead to actions that defy logic.

If you do overreact, what does this teach the child who has just done something they know is dumb and that they're ashamed of?

It basically teaches them to try to be more secretive

next time, so the parent doesn't have a conniption!

If parents respond with measured, thoughtful and even sympathetic words, children learn that it's safe to share their failures with their parents and that it may even be possible to glean insight from the parents into what is going on in their crazy lives.

Reacting during driving lessons

Let's take a simple example: driving. Most parents have the experience of teaching their child to drive. Kids become good drivers much faster if they're taught by calm adults sitting in the passenger seat as they run over curbs, drive too close to the edge of the road or hit speed bumps too hard. If the parent is constantly clutching the side handgrip as if their life depended on it or yelling at the child whenever he or she makes a little mistake, the child absorbs that tension and has a hard time learning to relax.

And then the child gets his or her license and ends up scraping the entire length of the car on a bicycle bollard while driving up a narrow pedestrian alley late at night because his buddy dared him to…

"What were you thinking? Why were you driving on a pedestrian pathway?!!! Do you have a brain?!!"

Oops. That is not the right way to respond.

"So… I'm glad you're okay. The pedestrians were okay, right? No damage to the bollard? I guess you have to think about how you're going to pay for the repairs and the ticket the policeman gave you; what do you think?"

This kind of response invites the child to participate

in dealing with the consequences of his or her actions. This kind of thinking helps the child develop the prefrontal cortex (which is the goal, by the way) and hopefully makes him or her think twice before accepting a friend's dare next time.

Reacting with drug/alcohol experimentation

Another example of when a parent is tempted to overreact is when the student experiments with drugs or alcohol for the first time. Maybe the parent smells alcohol on the child's breath or gets a call from the police late at night telling him that the child was present at a party where underage drinkers were partaking of alcohol.

A typical parental reaction goes something like this:

"I can't believe you'd do something like this! Don't you know that alcohol can destroy your life? You are grounded!"

Instead, what if the parent responded as follows:

"So, was it as exciting as you thought it would be? Did you feel pressured to do it, or was it your own choice? How do you think you'll proceed from here? Anything I can do to help?"

Again, the young adult is very soon going to have to make his own decisions about drinking. When he or she goes off to college, alcohol and drugs will be as available as water and bread. If parents have placed prohibitions without explanation, young people often rebel in college and go off the deep end in their experimentation, sometimes leading to wasted years.

In the case of illegal substances, parents need to

know the attitude their kids have toward them and maintain communication to make sure the child doesn't make bad choices.

Reacting to adolescent grunginess

Parents also sometimes have a hard time with the basic grunginess of the adolescent period. So many forces toy with the bodies and minds of adolescents that it would be miraculous if the young adult didn't feel mood swings, times of mental weirdness, depression, etc.

As adults, parents can forget what these times were like and develop impatient attitudes toward their kids.

"Why can't this kid get out of bed in the morning? I thought I'd taught him how to put his dishes in the dishwasher; he leaves stuff all over the place these days! He's worn the same shirt three days in a row; can't he smell himself?"

I know I've had times when I am just frustrated over something that seems like it should be simple. "Is it that hard to put the kleenex in the trash can after you use it? This is the 50th time I've told the kid!"

Just realizing that the adolescent time of life is what is to blame, not the child, can help the parent react with a little more patience and forgiveness. There *will* be a time when the child can clean his bathroom without being asked, wash his own clothes or throw his kleenex in the trash consistently, but it may not happen during this time when tumultuous oceans of growth hormones are swamping his psyche.

Reacting to dating/sexuality issues

And then there's the issue of the opposite sex... Whether your child is a young man or a young woman, sexual activity has dangers associated with it. Both men and women can get sexually transmitted diseases. Young women can get pregnant. The emotions and jealousies that revolve around relationships can lead to everything from physical fights to depression. In the midst of all this, it's easy for parents to freak out and discourage kids from any interaction with the opposite sex in fear of unwanted consequences. Alternately, parents can just give up and assume their kids are going to be involved in sexually dangerous active, and there's just nothing they can do about it.

Adults, too, struggle with issues of sexuality, so we should be the first to commiserate with our kids who are dealing with these issues for the first time. Sexuality is a great delight of life, but it can also be fraught with danger to the body and the emotions if it's not the right time for it. I believe this is one area where parents need to build a few more boundaries for their adolescents, especially when they're younger.

In general, dating and the potential of sexually charged situations that could lead to risky behavior is a topic about which parents and kids have a hard time communicating. Kids don't want to even think that their parents "do that," and parents tend to feel embarrassed talking about it. Because of this, parents often just don't mention sexuality and pretend the child is not a sexual being. This reaction is basically a parental abdication of the responsibility to protect their children in this area.

Rather than being passive, parents can pre-empt problems by having frank discussions about sexuality with their kids. One thing that helped us was to find some age-appropriate, short books on sexuality that the kids could read and that we could then discuss. The series we found had an age-appropriate 4th grade version, a 7th grade version, and a 9th grade version. By revisiting the topic every few years, we made it much more normal to talk about. If kids have correct information about how sex works, what the possible consequences of premarital sex are, and, according to our family's faith tradition, the value of waiting until marriage before having sex, they can make informed decisions.

I know the idea of waiting until marriage for sex may sound outmoded or overly religious to many people, but, regardless of faith tradition or lack of faith tradition, it's an idea that the world needs to reconsider. Developing strong friendship during dating is a much stronger foundation for a long-term relationship than uninformed experimentation in sexuality, especially since the power of the sex drive can actually lead young people away from communicating and turn every date into a physical encounter. When two people who have developed a strong friendship relationship commit themselves to each other in marriage, it provides a safe place to learn and explore the sexual relationship without fear of unwanted pregnancy or STDs, especially if both people have avoided sexual relationships previously.

Although you want your kids to be able to make their own decisions about dating, this is another area where you can influence things in an undercover or peripheral manner, especially when they're in the 12-15 age range.

Before kids get their driver's licenses, you are the main transportation for them. Because of this fact, you can encourage dates in public places like restaurants, movies, etc. You can coordinate with other parents to encourage double dating or going out with groups of friends to places where there are a lot of people. You can invite your child's boyfriend or girlfriend to do things with the family: come along on a family camping trip, hang out for 4th of July fireworks, or just come over for dinner and a family movie night.

Likewise, you can discourage kids going to parties at homes where parents are not in attendance by simply being unavailable to drive them there. We also talk honestly with our kids about going to unsupervised parties where alcohol is available as being dangerous situations that we'd prefer they didn't frequent.

By the time kids get their driver's licenses, parents need to have built open lines of communication with kids about dating and the dangers of letting hormones go wild since the autonomy created by being able to drive gives adolescents many more options for being alone with a member of the opposite sex. If you've built the right kind of openness in conversation with your kids about sexuality, the conversation could go like this:

"Hey Dad, I'm going on a date with Diana tonight to the movies. Then we're thinking of going to Chad's house for a few hours."

"Okay. Are Chad's parents going to be home?"

"I'm not sure."

"Well, I'd like you to check on that."

"If they're not, am I not allowed to go?"

"You are old enough to make your own decision in this case, but I think you need to be careful being alone late at night with your girlfriend. You don't want to get into a situation where the hormones can lead you into risky behavior."

"I understand. I think it's going to be a group at Chad's house just playing some video games."

"All right. Well, check on the parent situation and let me know. As usual, let us know if you're going to be out past 12:00."

"Okay. Thanks, Dad."

In any case, the parent's proper reaction to issues of relationships and sexuality is to place some boundaries, provide information, and then be available with compassion and without judgment to talk if (and when) kids make mistakes.

Whether responding to student driving, alcohol experimentation, adolescent grunginess, dating situations, or any of a myriad other situations, calm and measured parent reactions are key to maintaining good communication with your kids.

Limbic Lows

Dopamine-inducing activities lead to great highs. After scoring the winning touchdown or playing that violin solo in the concert, the adolescent can feel the healthy drug high for days.

But, the adolescent's body is awash in all kinds of hormones and is growing and changing in awkward lurches. As much as there are awesome mountaintop experiences in adolescence, there are also "pit of despair" feelings. And sometimes the switch from mountaintop to pit can happen within minutes.

Without a developed prefrontal cortex, many kids have no way to rationally process the idea that the low feeling will go away soon. Instead, it feels like they will be lost in darkness forever. This is where a parent's presence can be useful.

When you see your child groveling in the pit of despair, look for ways to move them toward something positive. This is not always easy while maintaining a position on the periphery, but it can sometimes be accomplished by encouraging connection to mentors or group involvements of some kind. I have seen many situations as a teacher where kids who are depressed are able to get out of their depression by having a significant experience with their friends by going on a school activity or a synagogue's summer camp or getting involved in a school club. I've also seen many kids emerge from the depths through interaction with mentors. Having a mentor show interest in you makes you feel valued and can sometimes help when you're down.

I remember one student named Craig who was going through a tough time in his life and was quite down. He was in my journalism class and would sometimes just come into my room and lie down under a table. I would try to talk with him, but he was just going through a low period and responded to my attempts with monosyllables. I was not the right mentor for him at that time.

What got him out of it was when a football coach noticed him walking around campus and said he had the right body type for a lineman and should try out for football. He did. Playing the game, having a mentor and being part of the team became a joy of his life that transformed his whole attitude. Even in journalism class, he became motivated to become the sports editor and left the funk behind. Although mentors or activities can pull people out of depression, there are times when it's necessary for a parent to leave the periphery.

As described in chapter 5, we took the risk of removing our 14-year-old son Justin from his peer group and transplanting him into a small concrete apartment in Ningbo, China with his parents and little sister and brother – not exactly the kind of situation a young adult who is in the process of differentiating from his parents gets excited about.

Although Justin experienced the dopamine highs of living in a strange culture, learning a new language, eating chicken heads and frogs' legs, etc., he also fell into despairing periods much more frequently than the other children.

I remember sitting with my wife at the end of a long day of dealing with Justin's depressed state. He had been unable to get out of bed and refused to go to school which required his sister to make the trip across the city to the Chinese school by herself despite my attempt to force Justin to go with some authoritarian parental bluster that had fallen flat. He barely ate anything throughout the day, and in the evening was lying on his bed in a darkened room staring at the ceiling.

As we discussed his situation in the other room, we felt low ourselves and were even entertaining the idea that we might have to return to America before the year was finished if Justin's despondency turned into some kind of clinical depression.

After talking about the situation and seemingly getting nowhere, I went into Justin's room and just lay down on the bed beside him. I didn't say anything. He told me to go away. I didn't. I just continued to lie on the bed beside him, saying nothing.

After 30-40 minutes, he asked me why I was lying there, so I asked him why he was lying there? Slowly, we began to talk. He expressed his sense of being in a dark pit. I asked him if going back to America would help. He was definitely against that since it would seem like he had ruined the year for the family.

In the end, we didn't come to any kind of solution or great turning point. This scene repeated itself several more times over the next few weeks. One thing I discovered, however, would get Justin out of his funk at times. He had always enjoyed running; in fact, the past year Justin had been one of the top runners on his school's cross-country team.

I am also a runner and annually run a half marathon to force myself to stay in some semblance of shape as I get older. In an attempt to get Justin out of his pit, I asked him if he'd like to train with me for a half marathon, a distance he'd never done before. As a cross country runner, he had regularly run 5K events, and he had done training runs of 6-7 miles, but he had never run 13 miles in a competition. After a little searching (since running competitions are not a big part of Chinese society), we discovered that there was a half marathon run each year in May with part of the trail going on the Great Wall of China. What a potential dopamine high!

Justin agreed to train with me, so we'd venture out along the riverside and through the city streets for semi-regular runs. As we moved through the year, Justin's funks became less frequent, and as we travelled north to Beijing for the Great Wall Half Marathon in May toward the end of our year in China, we discovered that conquering the Great Wall Half Marathon was symbolic for Justin conquering his depression.

I didn't really know it at the time, but I had intuitively provided Justin with a healthy, dopamine-inducing goal that helped him break out of his pit of despair.

Now this may seem like it goes against the idea of parenting from the periphery described in Chapter 3. That's true. I was definitely stepping inside the periphery, lying on the bed with Justin, and walking (or running) with him through the difficulty.

Even though staying on the periphery is the regular position for the parents of the adolescent, there are times when we must step inside the circle.

When Do You Leave the Periphery?

Before we can discuss the situations where the parent should leave the periphery, we need to clarify in which situations parents should not leave the periphery.

Tempted to leave periphery, better to stay

First of all, many parents feel it is necessary to leave the periphery when students grades begin to drop. Typical parental responses to dropping grades are grounding the kids until their grades come up or perhaps taking away some privilege like the cell phone or the use of the car. Prohibitions typically depress the students or lead to anger and rebellion rather than acting as a catalyst for positive change. Instead, the first step should be to remain on the periphery and try to get mentors involved.

A better response to dropping grades is to discuss privately with the teacher (the mentor) how things are going and ask the teacher to encourage the student to do better work. After all, that's the teacher's job – to teach. If the grades continue to fall, some open discussion with your child about how things are going in school, if there's something you as a parent can do to help, etc. is appropriate, but maintain the onus of learning on the student. If the parent steps in and tries to micromanage, it will not help the student learn how to manage the work him or herself. And please don't do the homework for the child. You want the grade to reflect the student's skills and knowledge, not yours!

A second area that does not usually warrant leaving the periphery is relationships. Love is an area of life that each of us has to figure out. The process of understanding how to love and be loved is almost invariably messy. Some parents prohibit kids from dating or highly restrict the kinds of social interactions kids can have with the opposite sex. The problem with this tactic after the age of 16 is that kids can drive and have a lot of freedom to interact with the opposite sex despite whatever prohibition you may have put in place. In addition most kids will soon go away to college where they will have no parental boundaries whatsoever. Then, being away at school with no prohibitions and no ancillary brain (yours), the student is at risk of doing something really harmful. It's better to stay on the periphery while letting kids learn some of the joys and pitfalls of dating before they get into the completely free atmosphere of college.

This is also true about alcohol and drugs. Parents should let kids be in situations where they feel the peer pressure to use alcohol and drugs, but ease them into these situations by first controlling the type of situations where they might encounter illicit substances, and by discussing the kind of pressure they'll receive throughout the process. A conversation could go like this.

"Dad, I'd like to use the car to go to a party at my friend Denali's house tonight."

"Do you know if there will be alcohol there?"

"We're all underage, Dad!"

"Of course, you are. That never stopped anyone from drinking when it's available. Have your friends ever pressured you to drink when you go to a party? They certainly did when I was a kid."

"What did you do in those situations, Dad?"

"I asked for a Coke instead, but I was kind of known as the athlete who didn't indulge in such things, so it was a little easier for me to say no."

"I only had it happen once, but I just told them I wasn't interested."

"That's great, but realize if there is alcohol at this party, you could be pressured to drink, then you'd need to drive home which would put you at risk of a car accident or getting caught for drunk driving, too. If you drink enough, it could impair your driving ability and lead to someone getting killed. You can always call me at any hour to come and get you rather than drive under the influence."

"I know all that, Dad. I will not drink anything tonight, and I'll even make sure I take the keys away from anyone who drinks and tries to drive home."

"You'd be showing yourself to be a good friend if you have the guts to do that. I'm fine if you go as long as you're thinking about the situations you could find yourself in."

"Okay. I will."

Of course, there is an exception to the above scenario with drugs and alcohol if your child has a track record of abuse. In that case, it is definitely time to step inside the periphery and help your child avoid hurting himself or someone else.

So, when do you leave the periphery?

In general, the main rule for when you need to step inside the periphery is if your child is *in danger of harm*. If they are getting into drugs, alcohol, gangs, other risky behaviors that could kill them, you will need to step in and cut off the behavior.

Unhealthy friend groups

Although it may feel like you're getting too nosy, it's important for parents to know the people who are influencing their children. Pay attention to the types of kids your child likes to hang out with. Again, it may feel like you're being too intrusive, but the smart parent tries to subtly influence the child away from groups who will influence them negatively.

An obvious example of this is if your children start to get into relationships with kids who are in gangs. Although the school where I have taught for 25 years didn't have problems with gangs, the first school where I taught for two years was an inner city school with a lot of gang problems. Each of my first two years, a student was killed: the first in a knife fight, the second with a gunshot. There are serious repercussions to gang involvement, and your child getting involved in a gang might be a reason to have your child go to a different school or even for a family to relocate to a different community.

A more subtle example is when your child gets involved with a group of kids who are completely unmotivated. At my school, this group ranges from ordinary kids with negative attitudes to those who get into doing marijuana and feel like the most important thing in the world is to sit on the beach and watch the ocean move around. Even if no drug abuse is involved, there is a certain segment of the population that hates school, badmouths anyone who tries hard, and generally seems to make apathy into a virtue. It's possible, especially when your kids are in the younger range (11-14) to steer your kids quietly away from this kind of crowd without using draconian prohibitions.

The secret is in focusing on positive relationships rather than the negative ones. Since you are still usually the child's transportation at that age, you can actively encourage your child to hang out with kids who have more motivation in life. For example, if you meet a family with kids who are positive role models, ask that family over for dinner, drive your child to activities that involve those friends, etc. There's no guarantee your child will click with the kids you want them to, but at least you're giving them an opportunity to do so. And if they do develop friendships, do whatever you can to encourage those friendships.

Notice that in this minor leaving of the periphery, you

are actively trying to influence your child's friendships, but you're still doing it quietly. If you have to leave the periphery, do it ninja style if possible.

Drug or alcohol addiction

An area where parents need to step very overtly into the circle is when the child gets addicted to drugs or alcohol. Some indications of addiction are identical to symptoms of adolescence in general: mood swings, depression, drops in grades, or other behavioral problems. Maybe that's because the vicissitudes associated with adolescence actually are tied to addiction to interior limbic drugs.

There are, however, more specific signs that parents need to recognize that can signal illicit drug or alcohol addiction. They fall into two categories: physical signs and drug paraphernalia.

Most high school teachers know that when kids show up at school regularly with bloodshot eyes that they hide behind sunglasses (even in a dark classroom), it is often a sign of marijuana, cocaine or alcohol use. Dilated eyes can be a sign of marijuana, alcohol, or amphetamine use while opiate use (like heroin) can constrict the pupils. If your child suddenly becomes sleepy all the time, has shakes or tremors, or has multiple unexplained nosebleeds, these could also be signs of drug abuse.

If you find your child in possession of drug paraphernalia, this is also a pretty clear sign that they are involved in illegal drug activity. Paraphernalia can include things like pipes or bongs, butane torches for crack or marijuana dabbing, porcelain bowls, hypodermic needles, vials, balloons, etc.

In addition to physical signs and drug paraphernalia, major personality changes can also be a tip-off of drug abuse. Although poor grades, rebellious behavior or apathy can be signs of normal adolescence, if these are major changes in behavior for your particular teen, pay attention to the possibility of drugs playing a part.

When drug addiction is the problem, find professional help. Your junior high or high school's counseling department can usually direct you to drug rehab programs if you don't know of resources in your community.

Clinical depression

As I related above in chapter 9, our son experienced some deep bouts of depression when we were in China. Although Justin had many good days in China, his low periods at times reached close to the level of clinical depression. In any case, it became serious enough that we felt we needed to get inside his circle and help pull him out of the murky pit.

According to the National Institute of Mental Health, clinical depression is defined as "a common but serious mood disorder. It causes severe symptoms that affect how you feel, think, and handle daily activities, such as sleeping, eating, or working. To be diagnosed with depression, the symptoms must be present for at least two weeks."

In a 2016 study the American Academy of Pediatrics found that the rate of clinical depression among youth aged 12-20 has increased significantly between 2005 and 2014 without a corresponding increase in those getting treatment, so parents need to be aware of this mental health issue.

Suicidal thoughts can also accompany depression, so, if your child exhibits symptoms of depression that carry on for weeks and months, you need to step in and get them help. This should include talking to your child's doctor, but sometimes what is needed is just for someone to be there. The strange thing about depression is that your child may very well push you away and say that they don't want you around, and yet inside they really do want you to be there. Sometimes cajoling the depressed teen into some interesting activity can pull them out of their funk; other times, nothing seems to help, but just hanging out with them can lessen their sense of doom.

Always remember to tell them that things *will* change. To the depressed teen, it seems like they will never be able to escape it, but there is always light at the end of the tunnel.

Eating disorders and cutting

Eating disorders and self injury are two behaviors that definitely require parents to come inside the periphery to get professional help for their kids. Eating disorders include anorexia (starving oneself), bulimia (throwing up or purging food from the body), and compulsive overeating. Self injury involves deliberate hurting of the body including cutting, burning or biting oneself. It's not uncommon for eating disorders and self injury behaviors to occur together.

If you notice your child losing weight, refusing to eat, seeming to be fixated on weight issues, regularly exhibiting scratches or bite marks or habitually wearing long sleeves even in hot weather, they could be dealing with an eating disorder or a self injury disorder. In these cases, seek professional help. Start with the pediatrician who can refer you to the proper mental health expert.

These kind of behaviors usually originate from deeper problems with stress, abuse, etc. and require both sustained involvement of the parents as well as health care professionals.

Cyber-problems

As a final example of things that require leaving the periphery of the adolescent's life to get more closely involved, I want to touch on the dangers connected with cyberspace and online activity. This is a complicated and daunting issue, especially for those of us who grew up before the internet was even a thing.

If you were born before 1990 or so, you don't naturally think of yourself as an online being as well as a physical being, but those born after 1990 are so used to living online that their online life is as important to them as their physical life. I don't mean this facetiously.

Kids create an image of themselves online that is always morphing as they grow and develop. They play online with their friends. They gather in groups to study online. They meet people and decide to date after online interaction. They carefully curate their online image and care highly how people respond to it. They immediately consult google for any question, factual or subjective, in order to decide what they think about an issue.

Despite all this, recent research shows that there is a causal link between time spent on social media and depression. The more time kids spend online, the more depressed they are. This is interesting because use of social media and the various activities kids do on phones also produce dopamine highs. This kind of activity can produce an unhealthy dopamine addiction, so it becomes hard for them to say no to that little notification sound that they have programmed into their phones. This is an addiction to a pleasure that depresses!

The issue of the depressive effect of constantly being online is definitely a cultural problem that needs to be addressed in a book much longer than this one, but I believe parents need to start well before kids become teenagers, making strong rules about screen use and considering how they can help their kids lessen online time. The parent is often the one paying for the phone or computer or ipad, so it's completely reasonable to say, "I'm paying for it, so I will set the rules for how it's used." That being said, remember that teens will respond best if you include them in the discussion of how and when to use devices.

"Research shows that the more time you spend on social media, the more depressed you become, so that's why we feel like we should place restrictions on our use of technology."

"Yeah, Dad, but you use it a lot, too."

"That's true. These restrictions are for me, too. I don't want to get depressed either, and I'd love it if you would point it out if you feel like the screen is preventing me from communicating with you well. What do you think is reasonable as far as screen time goes?"

"My friends can use it any time they want."

"Do you see kids comparing themselves to others online, feeling bummed because they aren't invited to the party they see online, getting depressed because their profile just isn't what they want it to be, etc.?"

"Yeah, but…"

"It's not only the depression problem, but being on the screen prevents people from reading books, exercising, and doing other things that are healthy for them. How about if we say we use our phones during the day until after school or work, then put them away in the evenings after dinner? Maybe the exception will be if you have a study group that you need to be part of. What do you think?"

"I guess that's okay."

"Let's give it a try, then re-evaluate after a month of so."

Not all online time negative

I personally believe that not all online time is the same. Students spending time on social media comparing themselves to the images their friends are putting up and eavesdropping on conversations that reveal activities they're not involved in is almost always negative. Playing video games can be healthy when done with friends for reasonable amounts of time. Research and communicating with people in meaningful ways (not playing the comparison games of social media) seem pretty innocuous to me.

Since technology influences our family lives, work lives, and leisure lives, as our culture continues to "technologize," a lot of research is going to be necessary to identify healthy and unhealthy internet activities as well as what is the optimal amount of time to spend with the face glued to the screen.

Helping your child to find the right balance of cyber-life and real life and the proper amount of time spent in each type of cyber-usage is an important area where stepping inside the circle is necessary because it's easy for people whose prefrontal cortex is undeveloped to be practically hypnotized by the cyberworld.

For example, the simple rule of requiring that phones charge outside one's bedroom at night can help kids not to be interacting 24-7 in cyberspace. Yes, you *can* buy an alarm clock that is just an alarm clock for a couple of dollars, so the cell phone *can* stay outside the bedroom. (The rule of leaving phones outside the bedroom is also healthy for adults and marriages, by the way.)

Cyber-bullying

In addition to putting some kind of limits on screen time, it's especially important for parents to leave the periphery in the situation of cyber-bullying.

According to the U.S. Department of Health and Human Services, cyber-bullying is:

> bullying that takes place over digital devices like cell phones, computers, and tablets. Cyberbullying can occur through SMS, Text, and apps, or online in social media, forums, or

65

gaming where people can view, participate in, or share content. Cyberbullying includes sending, posting, or sharing negative, harmful, false, or mean content about someone else. It can include sharing personal or private information about someone else causing embarrassment or humiliation. Some cyberbullying crosses the line into unlawful or criminal behavior.

Most cyberbullying takes place over social media apps like Twitter, Snapchat, Instagram, AskFM, WeChat, WhatsApp, Telegram, Kik, and even the ancient Facebook, but new apps are always being developed, and teens are usually the first ones to try to them out. So even when the parent has decided to enter the circle, it's often hard to know how to help.

The U.S. Department of Health and Human Services gives tips for parents on their stop-bullying.gov website:

While you may not be able to monitor all of your child's activities, there are things you can do to prevent cyberbullying and protect your child from harmful digital behavior:
- Monitor a teen's social media sites, apps, and browsing history, if you have concerns that cyberbullying may be occurring.
- Review or reset your child's phone location and privacy settings.
- Follow or friend your teen on social media sites or have another trusted adult do so.

- Stay up-to-date on the latest apps, social media platforms, and digital slang used by children and teens.
- Know your child's usernames and passwords for email and social media.
- Establish rules about appropriate digital behavior, content, and apps.

For parents who know nothing about how to patrol cyberspace, there is help online. (You, too, can google things!) Google "parental control software" and find some software to help you monitor your child's internet use without being too obtrusive. Although you may feel like a "big brother" watching your children online, this is an area where kids can get in real trouble and can use parental oversight.

On-line pornography is also something that can entrap young dopamine-seeking minds. Combine the technology dopamine and the sexual desire dopamine, and you have a powerfully addictive cocktail. Parental control software can help you see this kind of addiction developing, but conversation about this problem requires a lot of sensitivity and transparency. Most adults have had some kind of struggle relating to pornography, so sharing honestly with your kids can help them recognize and avoid problems.

A final cyber-danger to be aware of is the online predator. Since children's communication online is public, there is always the possibility that an online predator will attempt to harm your child. Talk to your child early about the dangers of online predation. Just like in real life, don't talk with strangers. Never reveal personal information like address or phone number to anyone online. Never agree to meet alone with anyone you met online. Make sure your kids know that predators exist and are completely okay with lying online to make you think they're someone that they're not. Finally, make sure you keep your eyes out for suspicious email or chat room time on your child's feeds and email.

If leaving the periphery, do it with respect

There are lots of other potential areas where parents may need to leave the periphery in order to keep their children safe.

One final comment, however, about stepping out of the periphery. If you have to do it, do it with respect and without treating your adolescent like a child. Remember what earlier chapters said about methods of talking with teens and parental reactions to avoid. Even if your child has been experimenting with drugs or has been getting to know kids in a gang, you need to communicate with them like you'd communicate with an adult. Rather than yelling at them or expressing disbelief that they could behave that way, treat them like the autonomous young adults they're becoming. "You have made a bad choice here, and I can't let you harm yourself. But you need to learn how to make the right choices, so you don't kill yourself. How can I help you with this?"

If you talk with your kids like adults, they'll learn to act like adults.

Final Thoughts

Where is the balance between protecting children and encouraging independence in young adults? As parents, our natural desire is to protect our kids, but they need to grow up and become responsible. After all, from age 18 on, they will be on their own to a great extent. In the best case scenario, they leave the family with solid values and an independent, competent spirit which will allow them to be successful in the real world.

As much as possible, therefore, we need to let 12-16 year olds be independent and make their own choices, even if it leads to failure. This is how they develop their prefrontal cortex and learn to trust their decision-making abilities, ultimately developing the skills they need to be independent. Parents need to facilitate this development of independence in the worst of conditions: at a time when their kids can literally not hear their voices.

In addition, the limbic system is powerful, leading developing adolescents toward risky activities, so, while adolescents are developing their prefrontal cortexes, parents need to be actively involved, albeit surreptitiously, watching what their kids lean toward, then encouraging healthy risk-taking, dopamine high-inducing behaviors that will give them the reward while letting them do the activity under some kind of adult or mentor supervision. In other words, parents need to help kids get addicted to healthy activities that can continue to benefit them into adulthood.

Parenting from the periphery does not mean being uninvolved in children's lives. In fact, it requires even more effort since you have to, first of all, recognize your need to change your parenting strategies from when children were young, and, second, add the element of "ninja parenting" where you attempt to influence while appearing not to influence by staying out of the center of things. It's not easy!

To summarize, keep these 12 things in mind if you want to try *Parenting from the Periphery*:

- Intentionally change your parenting style by moving from the lead to a peripheral position. Stay in the background whenever possible.
- Include your budding adult in decision making rather than telling them what to do or what is going to happen.
- Speak respectfully with your teen like you would speak with an adult; ask questions rather than use commands.
- Don't micromanage school work. Expect your child to stay on top of work.

- Encourage mentors in your child's life.
- Don't over-react to failures.
- Actively look for ways to get your child involved in healthy dopamine-producing activities.
- Encourage the healthy friendships your child initiates in whatever way you can.
- Be responsible to provide solid information and initiate frank conversations about sexuality.
- Be available for conversation, especially when your teen initiates it.
- Develop healthy family policies as regards to the use of technology that you evaluate and revise regularly.
- Don't hesitate to leave the periphery when your child's life is in danger whether from drugs, gangs, depression, eating disorders, etc.

The ideas I share in this book come from many years of working with adolescents, both in the classroom and in my own home. There is no guarantee they will work with your kids, but I have shared these ideas verbally with many parents and have heard about positive results from those who put them into practice.

My hope is that organizing these ideas in an easy-to-read book like this may help you in your parenting journey and help you develop your kids into healthy, independent young adults.

Chapter One Questions

1. In what ways have you seen the great highs and the great lows in your teen's life?

2. Whom do your teens tend to listen to during this time period?

3. Why do teens tend to listen more to someone other than their parents between the ages of 12-16?

4. As a parent, do you protect your children too much or try to make their choices for them?

5. Are you nostalgic for the time when your kids were little? Do you have a hard time letting your kids grow up? Are you pushing them to do what you want them to do without asking them what they want?

Chapter Two Questions

1. How old are children when the prefrontal cortex of their brain is mature?

2. Since the prefrontal cortex is the area of the brain where judgment and decision-making take place, why is the "hands off," permissive style of parenting not a good idea?

3. What role do the feel-good hormones like dopamine play in our lives as humans?

4. What particular dopamine addiction do teens have that adults don't?

5. Why is the combination of peer interaction and behavior like drug abuse or sexual experimentation a particular danger for addiction at this age?

Chapter Three Questions

1. What is the basic idea of parenting from the periphery?

2. Does parenting from the periphery mean that parents let their kids do anything they want?

3. Why do kids need an "ancillary brain"?

4. Where do you have the most difficulty retreating into the background: grades, romance, money going out with friends, or something else?

5. Why do teens respond better to flexible rules than rigid ones during this period of their lives?

Chapter Four Questions

1. In what way can dopamine be the friend of a parent who is parenting from the periphery?

2. What areas that offer dopamine highs does your teen naturally gravitate toward?

3. In what ways can you clandestinely encourage those activities that contain healthy dopamine highs?

4. Although sports are often incredibly healthy dopamine-producing activities, what danger sometimes accompanies success in sports?

5. What is the proper "parenting from the periphery" way to cheer for your child at a sporting event?

Chapter Five Questions

1. Why does traveling abroad for a lengthy trip with your family produce healthy dopamine highs?

2. Why is lack of cultural experience NOT a good excuse for keeping your family at home? In fact, why might lack of cultural experience be a good reason to go?

3. Based on what you've already learned in this book, why might your teenager have a little difficulty accepting the idea of going overseas, being separated from friends and having intense experiences with parents?

4. What does a year overseas do for a family?

5. Why should you run over to your computer right now and purchase a copy of *Jumping Out of the Maintream: An American Family's Year Abroad*? :-)

Chapter Six Questions

1. Since your teens can't hear your voice, which mentors could you subtly encourage your kids to talk to?

2. Why are mentors able to communicate with your kids when you can't?

3. How can you better use the resource of junior high and high school teachers? (If you know your child has a good relationship with a certain teacher, enlist that teacher to help you communicate in certain areas.)

4. What healthy dopamine activities does your child enjoy? Are there mentors you could enlist who would encourage that activity?

5. Does your child's school have academic clubs, music programs, service clubs, etc.? Quietly talk with the advisers of those programs and see if they'll reach out to your child (without telling them you initiated it!).

Chapter Seven Questions

1. Is the way you talk with your teen different than the way you talked with them when they were younger?

2. Do you tell your teens what to do or involve them in the decision making?

3. When making plans, does your teen feel like they are an integral part in the planning process?

4. Do you respect your teen's opinion enough to change your plans if he or she has a problem with them?

5. How do you think talking with your children like you talk with co-workers might help them feel respected?

Chapter Eight Questions

1. Have you ever overreacted when your teen did something stupid? How did your child respond to your overreaction?

2. How does a calm, measured, parental response to crazy actions encourage a teen to communicate?

3. Why is it important to lay the basic groundwork for communication about sexual issues when kids are still in their elementary years?

4. How can you prepare yourself for a calm reaction the first time your child experiments with alcohol or drugs? (It will probably happen. Are you prepared?)

5. When your toddler fell and skinned his or her knee, he or she immediately looked to you to see how you would react. If you looked too concerned, he or she would cry. Although teens are becoming young adults, your reaction still influences them. Remember that.

Chapter Nine Questions

1. How does the teen's undeveloped prefrontal cortex contribute to a tendency towards depression?

2. In general, why do teens have a tendency toward big mood swings?

3. How can you leverage a mentor's involvement to help your child when you see signs of depression?

4. Remember that teens need to be reminded that low times don't last forever. How can you creatively help your child understand that truth?

5. What significant experience could you plan for your child who has been feeling low lately (without being too obvious that you're planning it to help them)?

Chapter Ten Questions

1. Although the basic rule of parenting teens is to stay on the periphery of their lives as much as possible, when does the parent need to step inside the periphery?

2. In what areas are you personally tempted to enter the periphery, but probably shouldn't?

3. What signs might indicate your child is getting into serious drug use and could use intervention?

4. What should you do if your child (especially a girl) is dealing with regular depression and starts to wear long-sleeve shirts all the time, even when it's hot?

5. What conversations have you had in your family about social media and the use of phones/screens? Are you quietly monitoring their use of technology and stepping inside the periphery if serious bullying, sexting, social media comparison, etc. is occurring? Do you have a balanced relationship to technology yourself?

Works Cited

Chapter 2
Bergland, Christopher. "Why is the Teen Brain So Vulnerable." *Psychology Today*. Posted 19 December 2013. www.psychologytoday.com/blog/the-athletes-way/201312/why-is-the-teen-brain-so-vulnerable. Accessed 14 October 2017.

Steinberg, Laurence. *Age of Opportunity: Lessons from the New Science of Adolescence*. Houghton Mifflin Harcourt, 2014.

Chapter 10
National Institute of Mental Health (2016). "Depression." Posted October 2016. https://www.nimh.nih.gov/health/topics/depression/index. shtml. Accessed 30 December 2017.

Mojtabai, Ramin, et. al. "National Trends in the Prevalence and Treatment of Depression in Adolescents and Young Adults."American

Academy of Pediatrics, Nov. 2016, www.pediatrics. aappublications.org/content/early/ 2016/11/10/ peds.2016-1878. Accessed 19 July 2018.

Stop Bullying.gov. "Digital Awareness for Parents." U.S. Department of Human Services. Posted on 18 September 2017. https:www. stopbullying.gov/cyberbullying / Accessed 30 December 2017.

Acknowledgements

Writing a book is not something that happens in isolation. I would never have even started this without the encouragement of my wife, Caroline, who blazed the trail by writing her own book about our family's year living abroad in China: *Jumping Out of the Mainstream* (available on Amazon here: http://amzn.to/2yOBf46). Caroline has also been my proofreader, editor, artistic consultant, technology adviser and cheerleader. I love you, and am so thankful to God for putting you in my life.

I also want to thank my son Justin and daughter Erika for editing and comments as well as my son Luke for always being available to help at a moment's notice to magically solve any tech problem. What would we more mature people do without young people to give us advice on the latest trends and details of the technological world?

To my students, you guys are all awesome, and it has been my privilege to be a part of your lives as you progress into adulthood.

To parents of my students, thanks for entrusting them to

my care, and I hope this book contributes in some small way to making your parenting journey easier.

Two other friends, Robert Muni and Mako Minegishi also gave me significant feedback. To them I say, Asante and ありがとうございます, respectively!

To God, I thank you for life, breath, and the way you walk with me. I want this book to honor you.

About the Author

Dale DePalatis has worked in the field of education for over 30 years. In addition to teaching ESL in Japan and China, he has taught English Language and Literature to high school students in the Carmel Unified School District for over 25 years.

A graduate of Stanford University with a B.A. in English and Italian Literature and an M.A. in English Literature, Dale also loves languages and the exploration of different cultures. He and his wife Caroline have developed a venture called YourGlobalFamily, aiming to help parents raise globally-minded kids.

YourGlobalFamily

Parenting from the Periphery is part of a joint effort by husband-wife team Dale & Caroline DePalatis to create a platform dedicated to the goal of helping parents raise awesome, globally-minded kids. Together, they have spent over 25 years participating in and leading an outreach to international college, university and graduate students, scholars, wives, couples and families, mostly in Monterey, California, USA.

To find out more – especially how you can be a part – please visit our website, https://yourglobalfamily.com.

"A must read if you are going to travel with your family or travel by yourself abroad."

Jumping Out of the Mainstream:
An American Family's Year Abroad

Jumping Out of the Mainstream is the true story of an Amerian family taking a break from their ordinary life, making discoveries about themselves and the world, and growing closer in the process.

Take a journey to other lands without actually leaving your living room. But also, get inspired to realize you can do this as well with your family!

Jumping Out of the Mainstream is a swift, engaging read, with short, fast-moving chapters. It's also a 5-star read on Amazon. Available here: http://amzn.to/2yOBf46.

53047603R00057

Made in the USA
Lexington, KY
24 September 2019